AF594880

Every Word
Tells
A Story

For the five children who daily stretch my notions of what the young mind is capable of...
Artie and Albi, Lillia, Fenton and Dulcie

x

TRW

For Mum and Dad–without their love and support my goals would be even harder to achieve

IM

First published in 2022 by words & pictures,
an imprint of The Quarto Group.
100 Cummings Center,
suite 265D Beverly,
MA 01915, USA.
T (978) 282-9590 F (978) 283-2742
www.quarto.com

Editorial Assistant: Alice Hobbs
Editor: Helen Mortimer
Art Director: Susi Martin
Publisher: Holly Willsher

A CIP record for this book is available from the Library of Congress.

ISBN: 978-0-7112-7753-3

9 8 7 6 5 4 3 2 1

Manufactured in Guangdong, China TT072022

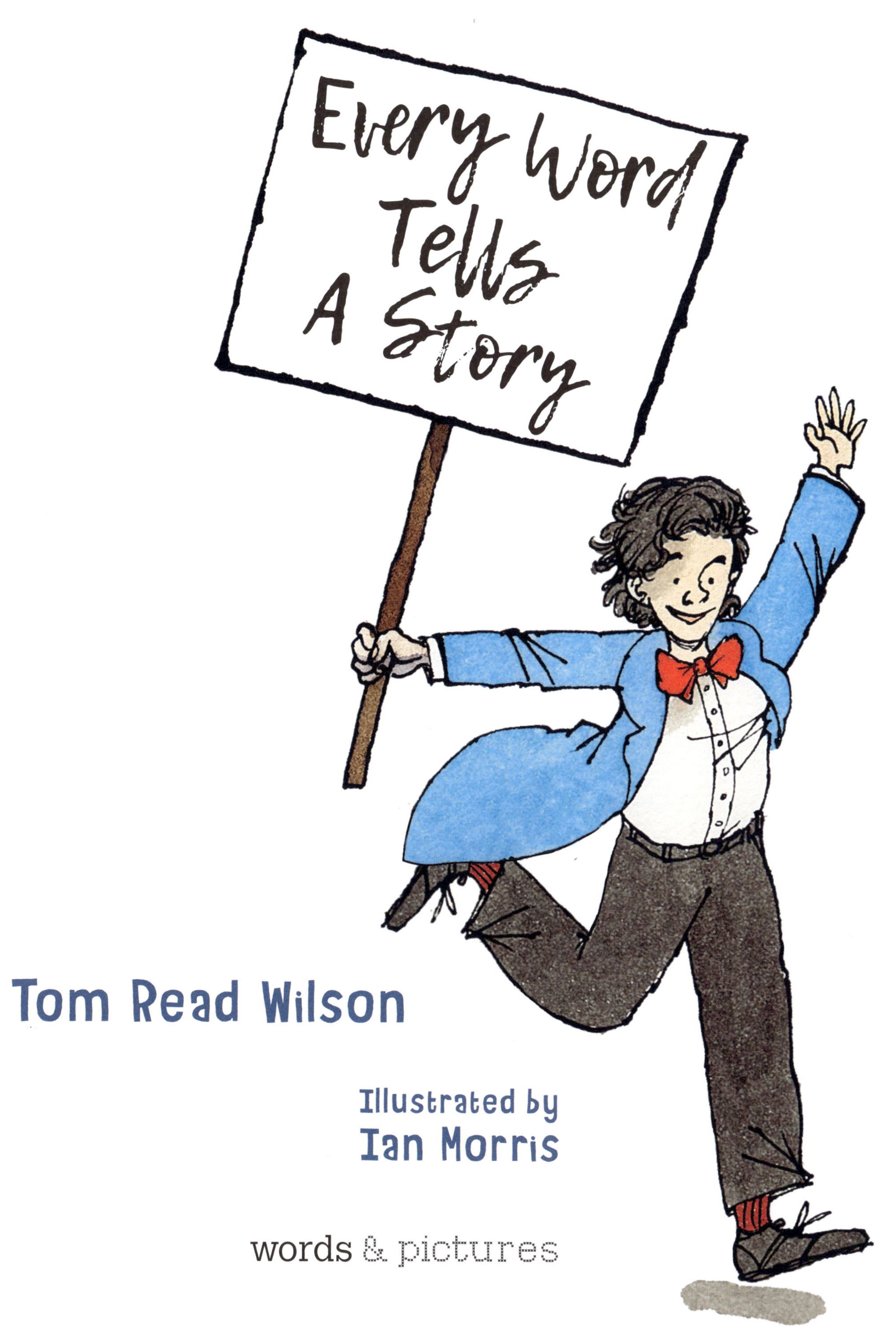

Every Word Tells A Story

Tom Read Wilson

Illustrated by
Ian Morris

words & pictures

Introduction

"Mama. Wow. Cake. Bug Ball." These were my nephew's first words. These words, I believe, tell you everything that is most important about him to this day. "Mama": his favourite person; "wow": the way he reacts to our dazzling world; "cake": his ceaseless delight in all kinds of bakes; and "bug ball": his love of music, since these words come from the song "The Ugly Bug Ball." I sang this to him so often that he referred to me as Bug Ball long before he started to call me Uncle Tom.

The words we choose to say, and the words we choose *not* to say, are one of the earliest indicators of our personalities. But words have personalities, too! In this book you will discover the personalities of a sprinkling of words from A to Z. As the title says, every word really does tell a fascinating story.

Who knows, you might even become part of a word's story. You might invent something and give it your own name. You might say something in an interesting way and all your friends begin to say it that way, too. You might find a favorite expression too long and clunky and come up with a shortened version. Or you might shrink an existing word.

Our language has always been shaped by individual tastes and personalities, as people find new ways of expressing ideas and using words. In this book I reveal a selection of my favorite word stories, but first...

How to use this book

For each letter of the alphabet, I have picked out four words. I start things off with a "star word" poem. The poem is accompanied by a handy table that summarizes the word's meaning and origins along with some other word facts that are related to the star word in all kinds of interesting ways. On turning the page, you'll find three more words whose captivating stories have caught my imagination.

The four featured words for each letter of the alphabet, along with the related words, are picked out in purple the first time they are used.

The word's source (from another language or a name, for example) is picked out in red.

The meaning of the source word is picked out in green.

Words in the English language have sometimes taken a journey from all over the world to reach our tongues.

Glossary

Throughout the book, you'll come across these specialized terms that are used by all lovers of words. These words are picked out in **bold** the first time they are used.

Abbreviation A shortened form of a word.

Acronym The first letters of a set of words, put together in such a way that they can be pronounced as an ordinary word: FOMO is "fear of missing out."

Clipping The part of a word remaining when some of it has been removed.

Coining A new, invented word.

Definition The meaning of a word.

Dialect A particular way of speaking or using words that belongs to a specific region or group of people.

Eponym A word based on the name of a particular person–real, fictional, or mythological.

Etymology The study of the origins of words.

Initialism If the letters from a set of words are put together and each letter must be separately pronounced, then it is an initialism. Most initialisms are formed using the first letters of words, such as FYI for "for your information." But there are many exceptions, such as TV, which takes its "V" from the middle of "television."

Lexical Anything to do with the words or vocabulary of a language could be described as "lexical."

Nickname A familiar and often funny word or phrase used to describe a particular person or thing.

Onomatopoeia Onomatopoeic words sound like the thing or action that they are used to name. "Cuckoo" and "plop" are both examples.

Portmanteau A word that blends the sounds and also combines the meanings of two others, for example "brunch," which comes from "breakfast" and "lunch."

Root The part of a word that can be traced back to an older language.

Synonym A word or phrase that means exactly or nearly the same as another word or phrase; for example "large" is a synonym of "big."

Vernacular
Everyday language.

Aardvark

Aardvarks, like pigs, have a lovely, long snout
For sniffing where termites and ants are about.
They snuffle at nighttime for all they are worth
And use their strong claws for digging the earth.
In Dutch Afrikaans we are given a clue
By splitting their name from one into two:
Aard is the earth and piggy is vark.
For only an earth pig eats ants in the dark!

Aardvark: A nocturnal badger-sized burrowing mammal found in Africa
Word origin: Afrikaans—a language similar to Dutch spoken in some parts of southern Africa
Meaning in source language: Earth pig
Etymologically speaking
The Old English word for **nose** is **snowte**. This is where **snout** comes from. It might also explain why so many words to do with noses start with the letters "sn." Snort, snore, snivel, sniffle, snuffle and snot are just some examples.
What's in a name?
The **guinea pig** is named after **Guinea** in West Africa, probably by mistake since it comes from South America and is a rodent, not a pig!

Ambulance

Wounded French soldiers in the 18th century would be treated in a hôpital ambulant or walking hospital. Pulled by horses, these really did go at a walking pace. When French and British soldiers fought side by side in the Crimean War, the word entered our language as ambulance. Luckily, they now go a lot faster. Unlike the contraption that you were probably pushed along in when you were just a babe. A stroller–which British people call a pram–makes it easy for an adult to ambulate (or walk) with a baby in tow!

Anemones are beautiful flowers that have wide, plate-like petals and come in oodles and oodles of cheerful colors. They love woodlands and the shade: they typically thrive in cool and breezy spots. No wonder their attractive name means daughter of the wind in Greek. They make their home in the places many flowers try their best to avoid.

Anorak

Would you wear an anorak for your wedding? Me neither, but the early anorak, or Greenlandic annoraaq, was in fact bridal attire made from beaded and oiled animal skins. By the 1950s anoraks were popular fashion items in Europe where the need for weatherproofing wasn't quite so great. A very chic poplin (strong, woven fabric) version even appeared in an issue of *Vogue* magazine in 1959. Yes, anoraks were quite literally in vogue!

Bloomers

Amelia Bloomer was born in New York in 1818, in May.
So now that you know her name and her dates
What else is there here to say?
She stood up for women and fought for their rights
By speaking and writing with passion.
And something important she had in her sights
Was bringing them freedom through fashion.
She campaigned for clothes that were roomy and loose–
A new kind of ankle-length knickers.
And, bearing her name, they were soon in wide use
In spite of some naysayers' snickers!

Bloomers: Loose-fitting ankle-length knickers

Word origin: Named after Amelia Bloomer (1818–1894)

Word first used: 19th century

Etymologically speaking

As you know bloomers are really just long knickers. But knickers is an **abbreviation** of **knickerbockers** and they, too, are named after somebody: Diedrich **Knickerbocker**, the invented narrator of Washington Irving's book, *A History of New York*. The Dutch settlers described in the book wore breeches, a sort of short trousers for horse riding, so Diedrich's surname became forever associated with this kind of legwear.

Did you know?

Bloomers are back! Yes, I keep seeing very attractive **yoga bloomers** which, just like Amelia's, are wonderful for dynamic movement. **Yoga**, incidentally, is a Sanskrit word meaning **union**, presumably of a focused body and mind.

Biscuit

I don't recommend this, but if you were to take a slice of leftover bread or cake and bake it a second time, the result would resemble what the Brits call a biscuit–that's a cookie to you and me! These days, there are simpler ways to make them, but the Latin bis coctusi, meaning twice baked, refers to this early method of making these crisp, srumptious morsels.

Bumf

If you like watching British TV (and who doesn't?), you may have heard characters talk about bumf when they're complaining about unwanted paperwork or scraps of old homework at the bottom of their backpack. It sounds like an invented word that was made up to sound silly, but don't let bumf fool you. Question it. Where did this odd term come from? It's a shortened word, or **clipping**, that indicates that these pieces of unwanted paper are about as useful as bum fodder! And what, may you ask, is bum fodder? It's toilet paper or anything else you use to clean your bottom!

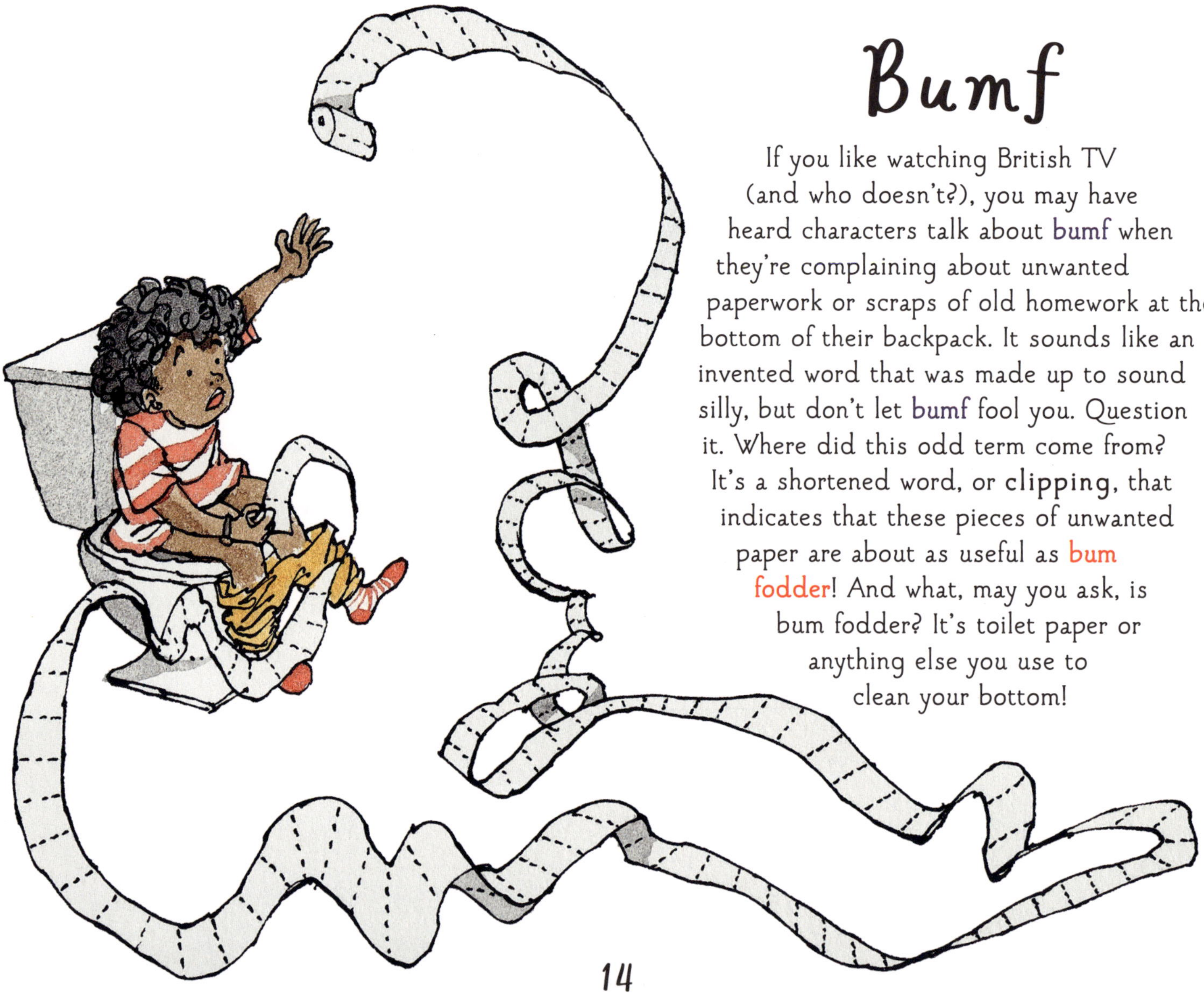

Bobby

Sir Robert Peel (1788-1850) was a Victorian known as "the father of English policing." He may be the only person in the world to have been Prime Minister twice and to have had both his names used as **eponyms**! Peel came first. After he had created the country's first modern police force, its officers were called peelers. Perhaps this made them sound as though they'd been sunburned or busy with the parsnips, so a shortened form of Sir Robert's first name was adopted instead, and in the UK people still call police officers **bobbies** today.

Chameleon

Chameleon comes from the Greek
For lion on the ground.
But it's a lizard, quite unique,
And makes no roaring sound.
In Ancient Greece they thought its casque
Looked rather like a mane.
Accordingly (before you ask)
That's how it got its name!

Chameleon: A lizard that is able to change color

Word origin: Ancient Greek

Meaning in source language: Lion on the ground

Etymologically speaking

Also, from the Greek **leon** comes **leonine**, a rather fancy way of saying **like a lion**. It's a gorgeous word to use when admiring human hair. In fact, I often remark in the presence of a dazzling mop, "Your mane is positively leonine!"

Did you know?

The biggest casque in animal history belonged to the **triceratops**. **Triceratops** means **three-horned face** in Greek. Some people believe its giant head housed 800 teeth!

Canapé

I do hope you have already sampled one of these tasty treats! If not, canapés are one of the culinary joys that await you. Very often, they are your favorite foods shrunk into individual, perfect, bite-sized prettiness, topped with a garnish to be served at parties: a baby **quiche**, a teeny pizza, or even a tiny pancake topped with sour cream and smoked salmon (or caviar if you're feeling really fancy!). Canapé is the French word for sofa. The idea translates to nibbles because of the notion of an elegant base topped with any number of delicious things, the way a sofa may be topped with all kinds of delicious people.

Clodhopper

Have you ever seen the funny way people trudge across a muddy field? They often widen their gait and start to walk a little like they've pooped in their pants. This is because they're clodhopping, or moving to avoid the clod. Clods are the lumps of mud, manure, and clay that you're apt to find in country fields. A clodhopper was someone who spent most of their time in fields of clod: a farmer, perhaps. Now it simply means someone who moves like they're hopping clod, even when they're walking in loafers down the street.

Clue

Long before the fairy tale where Hansel and Gretel left a path of breadcrumbs to find their way back from the witch's cookie cottage, in Greek mythology Theseus did a similar thing with a ball of thread called a clew. He had slain the vicious Minotaur who was waiting deep in a maze, but clever Theseus knew his perils wouldn't be over after the battle: he would have to find his way back out of the maze. The clew provided the clue, and that is precisely why this thread came to mean any kind of hint or guide.

Etymologically speaking

Another wildflower with an animal in its name is the **cowslip**, found across Europe. It doesn't have anything to do with a cow's lip but a **cow's slyppe**, an Old English word meaning **slop**, **slobber** or **dung**. The slyppe was a lovely, warm, nutty spot in which these flowers could thrive!

Did you know?

William Shakespeare was a fan! The world's most famous playwright penned some words for our toothy bloom: "O thou weed, who art so lovely fair"!

Dandelion

Once, in France, a common weed
Was named as dent de lion–
Or lion's tooth–when said at speed
Becoming dandelion.
And if you peer below the flowers,
The green leaves underneath
In any language–French or ours–
Do look as sharp as teeth!

Dandelion: A widely distributed weed of the daisy family

Word origin: Old French

Meaning in source language: Lion's tooth

Dinosaur

For my favorite prehistoric animal–the huge, vegetarian, majestic Diplodocus–dinosaur seems an ill-fitting name. It combines the Greek deinos or terrible and sauros or lizard. This might suit the gnarling, flesh-eating, bone-crunching Tyrannosaurus rex, but not dear old branch-chewing, tail-swishing, broad-footed Diplodocus.

Daisy

Like me, at nighttime, I suspect you are safely tucked up in bed. But if you're a wildflower, you don't have a bed, so the best way to be snug and protected at night is to wrap yourself up in your own petals. When you feel the warmth of the sunshine once more, you may unfurl your petals and reveal the "eye" of your flower. So a daisy's name is short for day's eye since its bright yellow center is revealed especially to greet the day.

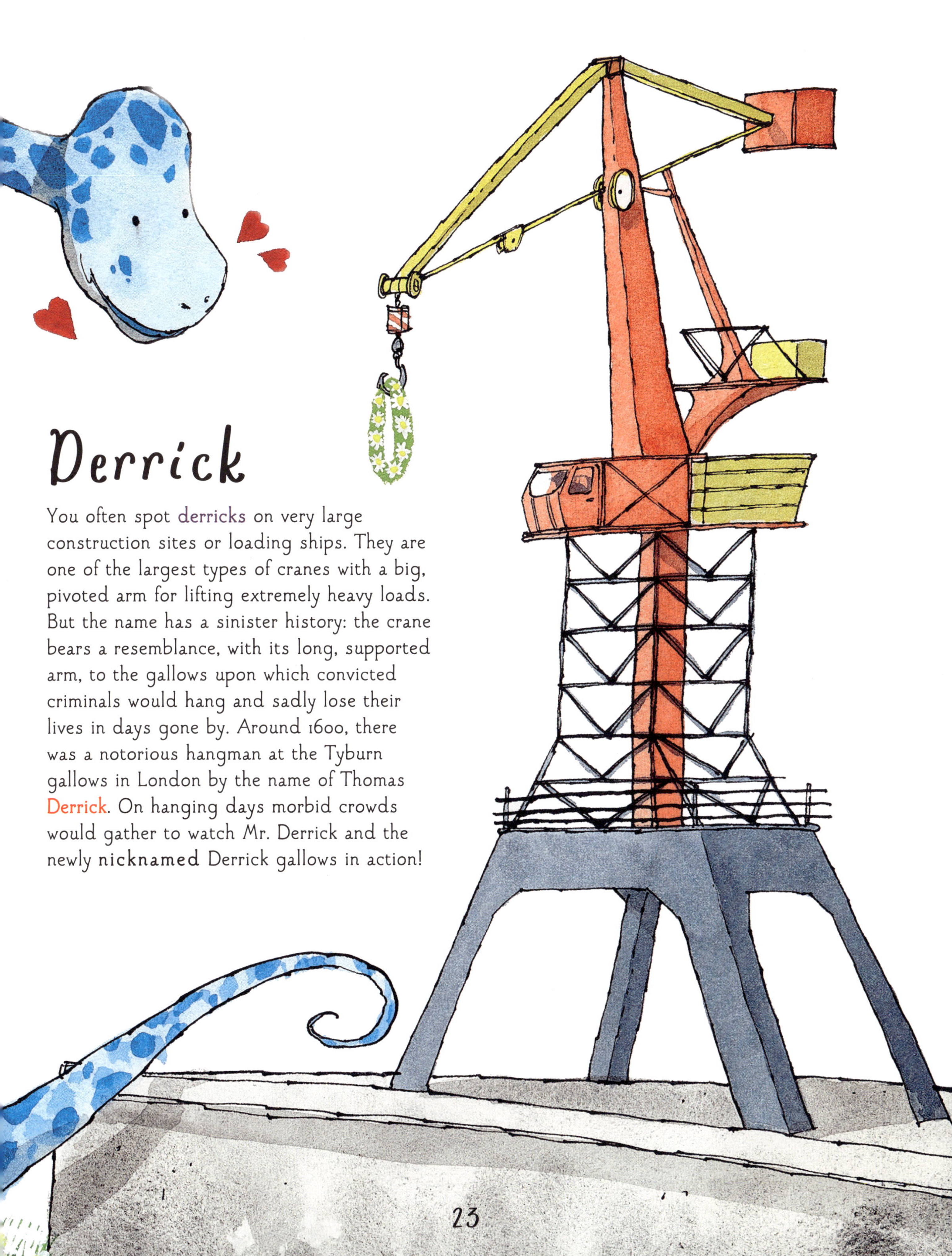

Derrick

You often spot derricks on very large construction sites or loading ships. They are one of the largest types of cranes with a big, pivoted arm for lifting extremely heavy loads. But the name has a sinister history: the crane bears a resemblance, with its long, supported arm, to the gallows upon which convicted criminals would hang and sadly lose their lives in days gone by. Around 1600, there was a notorious hangman at the Tyburn gallows in London by the name of Thomas Derrick. On hanging days morbid crowds would gather to watch Mr. Derrick and the newly **nicknamed** Derrick gallows in action!

Echo

Echo was a mountain sprite
Whom Zeus found very charming.
His wife thought this an awful slight
Her actions were alarming.
She took away sweet Echo's voice,
As tuneful as a bird's,
Condemning her (without a choice)
To echo others' words.

Echo: A repeated sound caused by the bouncing of sound waves

Word origin: Greek mythology

Who was she?
A nymph whose voice was reduced to repeating words that others said by a jealous goddess

Etymologically speaking

Another goddess who suffered from bouts of rage caused by jealousy was Athena. She couldn't accept that a mere mortal, **Arachne**, was a better weaver than she. So, Athena said, "If your weaving's so fine, you won't mind being turned into a creature whose only purpose is to weave!" And so, the first **arachnid** or **spider** was born!

Did you know?

Echo is a code word to represent the letter "E" used in radio communications. The whole alphabet, known as the NATO phonetic alphabet, is: Alpha, Bravo, Charlie, Delta, Echo, Foxtrot, Golf, Hotel, India, Juliet, Kilo, Lima, Mike, November, Oscar, Papa, Quebec, Romeo, Sierra, Tango, Uniform, Victor, Whiskey, X-ray, Yankee, Zulu.

Easel

The clue for a donkey, whenever it appears in my crossword puzzles, is invariably "beast of burden." Why? Because historically the poor old donkey's strong flat back was regarded as useful for burdening with all one's heavy luggage. Why am I talking about this to explain the word story of the easel? Because the structure that bears the weight of an artist's canvas takes its name from the Dutch ezel meaning donkey. It shares the donkey's dependable suitability for loading.

Euphemism

Sometimes it just feels too difficult to say certain words. Some may think this is silly. They are, after all, just words. But words like dead and sick, for example, are sometimes too uncomfortable for us to say–they refuse to leave our mouths freely. So we've invented lots of expressions to make them sound sweeter and these are called euphemisms, from the Greek eu for sweet or good and phēmē meaning speech. So instead of getting sick we're "off colour," "below par," or "under the weather." Instead of dying we might "push up daisies," "cash in our chips," or "kick the bucket."

Eavesdrop

You might have heard of eavesdropping (the art of secretly listening in on conversations) without having heard of eaves. I think the simplest way to explain eaves is to say they're that overhanging part of the roof under which bees may build their hives or birds their nests. Once upon a time, the ground underneath the eaves, where the rain would drop, was called the eavesdrop. If you were to stand awhile on the eavesdrop near an open window, you might just catch an interesting conversation never intended for your ears!

Flora

The Roman goddess Flora
Had the most wonderful powers.
Her husband was Zephyr, god of the breeze,
And here is why flora means flowers:
Zephyr would scoop Flora up in the air
And, flying sky-high, she would drop
Seed after seed into gardens below
To land in the soil with a plop.
Quick as a flash all the seedlings would sprout,
Each blossom a different shade,
And Flora and Zephyr would float down to earth
Admiring the blooms they had made.

Etymologically speaking

In Middle English **flower** in the sense of **the best part of something** was applied to the finest quality of ground wheat. It was not until the early 19th century that the spelling was changed to **flour** and the two words went their separate ways!

What's in a name?

Zephyr is the god of the breeze. We use his name as a **synonym** for breeze. In fact, I'm quite likely to say, on opening my front door to a strong breeze, "Goodness! It's zephyrous out!"

Flora: The plants of a particular region

Word origin: Roman mythology

Who was she?

Goddess of flowering plants

Friday

Our monthly calendar might be very Roman, but our weekdays are very Old Norse. Friday is short for Frigga's day. Like Venus in Ancient Rome, Frigga is the goddess of love in Norse mythology. Venus gives the French their word for Friday, which is "vendredi." No wonder Friday is date night! I always feel a great surge of romance from the pit of my tummy (funny place to feel it, I know) on a Friday. Thank you, Frigga!

Ferret

Ferrets have so many ways of grabbing their lunch. There are lots of options on the ground, but if they get bored of small, scurrying prey, they are very good climbers, so they can easily rob the contents of a bird's nest instead. They are not picky: they will steal the newly hatched chicks if they're there but if not, they will take the eggs. No wonder these ravenous robbers take their name from the Old French furet, meaning thief.

Frippery

Golly! How I love this word. Not least because it means the complete opposite of its **root**. In Old French frepe means rag. But frippery means fussy, unnecessary, grand decoration added to clothes, speech, or even your sitting room! The French started to play on this idea of rags and seemingly useless bits and pieces to describe bits of upmarket fussiness added to just about anything. It was ironic to start with but soon it stuck!

What's in a name?

Originally the **Goths** were not edgy teenagers in oversized black hoodies and skull rings. They were an ancient German people. The Goths had great style, eerie but beautiful, and their buildings started to be copied all over Europe. The word **Gothic** became associated with the spookiness of this style.

Did you know?

The gargoyle is probably the only grotesque creature I can think of that began life in architecture. All the others come from myths, fables, and legends. It is, therefore, completely unique!

Gargoyle: A decorated stone head that drains water from a roof

Word origin: Old French

Meaning in source language: Throat

Gargoyle

Architects love buildings; especially the features
That decorate old stonework and sometimes look like creatures.
On Gothic walls you'll often see, just below the gutter,
Faces spitting water out when rainfall starts to splutter.
These **gargoyles** take their name from French–
Gargoule means **throat**–their thirst they quench
By gargling lots and lots of rain
And acting as a kind of drain!

Grinch

It's woe to bend the stubborn back
Above the grinching quern,
It's woe to hear the leg-bar clack
And jingle when I turn!

I don't remember *that* in Dr. Seuss, you might well be thinking. You're right! These lines are from an 1888 poem by the author of *The Jungle Book*, Rudyard Kipling! A quern was a sort of hand mill, a bit like a pestle and mortar. Grinching referred to the sound and, I suspect, is a **portmanteau** of grinding and screeching invented by Kipling. How fitting, then, that Dr. Seuss's creature of constant griping and complaining should bear the name Grinch.

Guru

You might go to a fashion guru to steer your style, to a religious guru to steer your decisions, or to a fitness guru to aid your health. The word itself is ancient. Guru comes from Sanskrit (one of the world's oldest languages) and means weighty. Of course this does not refer to the gurus themselves being hefty, but that the nuggets of wisdom they impart carry such weight and impact, they may change your life and the choices you make.

Guillotine

Believe it or not, this terrifying device, which chops off heads, was designed to be kind! In the olden days, when criminals could be put to death in Europe, the ways of killing them were too gruesome to even mention here. During the French Revolution, many people were sent to the guillotine. A doctor, Joseph-Ignace Guillotin (1738-1814), said this razor-sharp, weighted blade would chop off the head so quickly and cleanly that there wouldn't be so much as a moment's pain. Mercifully, we'll never know!

Hippopotamus: A large semiaquatic African mammal with massive jaws

Word origin: Ancient Greek

Meaning in source language: River horse

Hippopotamus

A happy hippo loves its home:
A muddy stream or lake.
But when I say what hippo means
You'll think there's some mistake.
Potamos means river,
Which makes a lot of sense,
But hippo is a horse. A WHAT??
Please don't take offense!
A horse and hippo, after all,
Are not that far apart:
They both eat grass in great amounts
Which makes them want to fart!

What's in a name?

Of course the other famous aquatic horsey name is seahorse. Seahorses are small fish belonging to the genus **Hippocampus** which comes from the Ancient Greek **hippokampos**. We know that **hippo** means **horse** and **kampos** means **sea monster**!

Etymologically speaking

A certain horsiness is retained in many words in our language today. Famous horse races like the Preakness Stakes are still sometimes described as **hippic**, or horse-related, events. And **hippodromes**, which today can be any large space used for entertainment, such as concert halls or theatres, were originally round stadiums used for horse racing.

Hex

When it comes to witches, people divide into two camps: those that find them quite frightening, and those that find them glamorous and exciting. I'm squarely in the second camp. Which camp are you? Hexe is an Old German word for witch. But Americans transformed the word into what a witch does: casting a spell. So you might say, "I spent a whole day craving nothing but broccoli, as if I were hexed!"

Hoover

When electric vacuum cleaners were introduced, they were a marvel. William Hoover (1849-1932) ran a vacuum cleaner company in Ohio, and his product was so popular that in countries such as the UK, the brand name was soon being used for any carpet cleaning device—and they are still called hoovers today! When I was very little, my grandma seemed to be attached to her hoover, so I called her Granny Poover (I couldn't quite manage hoover). It sounds slightly better than Granny Vacuum Cleaner!

Hygiene

Hygeia was a Greek goddess and daughter of Asclepius, the god of medicine. His symbol–a snake–was shown sipping from a bowl of Hygeia's healing potion and the combined image has been used to represent pharmacies ever since. Just as Hygeia was a great help to her father, the word she gave us–hygiene–became a vital part of health care when two of the main causes of plague and other diseases were dirty water and unclean bodies.

Insect: Invertebrate animals with bodies divided into three parts and six legs arranged in pairs

Word origin: Latin

Meaning in source language: Cut into

Insect

You'd have to be cruel to slice up a bug!
But that is how insect translates:
In Latin in's into and sect means to cut.
Is cruelty just one of our traits?
Don't panic–it's merely a way to describe
Bodies divided in three:
Abdomen, thorax, and head all combine
In earwig or beetle or bee!

Etymologically speaking

The **etymology** of insect is curious, but not half as curious as that of **bug**! It may be from the Middle English **bugge** meaning **something frightening**. This is where we get words like bugbear, an object of fright, and probably even the bogeyman!

What's in a name?

My favourite word is...wait for it...**papilionaceous**! It means like a butterfly since **papilio** is Latin for **butterfly**. I think it's hugely versatile: you could say a very light-on-their-feet ballet dancer moves papilionaceously, or, even more adventurously, you might describe Clark Kent's rapid change into Superman as a papilionaceous transformation!

Iceberg

In a way, the word iceberg has a hidden meaning. A berg in Dutch is a mountain. We only see the summit of the ice mountain described in the name because these amazing frozen bodies stretch just as far, if not further, below the water's surface as above.

Ink

There were all kinds of ways to write before ink became universal. Engraving on tablets and branding were both very popular. Branding involved heating metal symbols and burning them into wood. The Greek word enkaiein means to burn in, and with the result being a kind of sooty lettering, you can see how ink found its name in the enk of enkaien.

Iris

You may be reading this book on your own, or you may have some lovely person reading it with you. If it's the latter, turn and look at their eyes. Closer. The colored part is called the iris. There might be a dominant color: brown, blue, green, gray. But look very carefully, until you're almost nose to nose, and I promise you'll find at least four more shades. The more you look the more you will find. And that is why the name for this part of the eye comes from the Greek iris meaning rainbow.

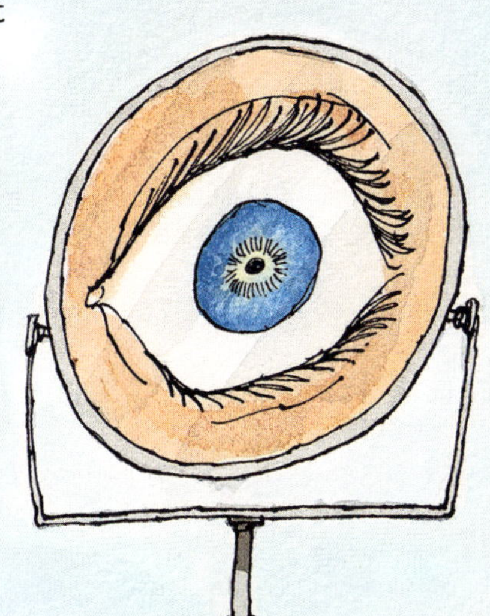

Etymologically speaking
Another word that has come to English from Swahili is **safari**. In Swahili **kusafari** means **to travel**, even just catching a bus!
Did you know?
My other favorite game is **Scrabble**. Just like Jenga, which has an instructional title, Scrabble is so called because one must scrabble around collecting letters.

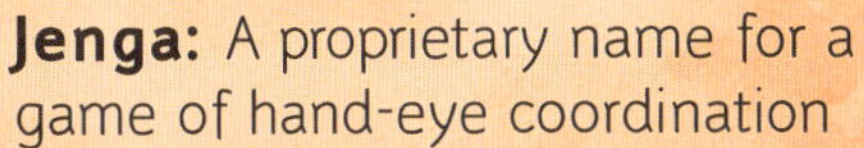

Jenga: A proprietary name for a game of hand-eye coordination

Word origin: Swahili—a language that is spoken in East Africa

Meaning in source language: To build

Jenga

Jenga! Here's a dauntless claim:
Jenga is my favorite game!
To further praise its skilled creator
Giant Jenga's even greater!
If it's a game you haven't played,
The rules are easily conveyed:
Build a tower, block by block,
Take one out and watch it rock
As you place it on the top
Pray your edifice won't flop!
The name of Jenga fits ideally:
Meaning build–but in Swahili!

Jackal

We don't have many mammals that are named for the noise they make: the jackal is a rare exception. In Turkish çakal means howler, and this wild dog's howl is extremely useful to other, bigger predators like lions. When jackals yelp, smaller animals leap and fly and scurry in terror, often, right into the drooling jaws of the lions, who are always on standby. And once the lions have eaten, jackals will scavenge the leftovers, so both animals benefit from the bark!

Juggernaut

A juggernaut is an unstoppable force that crushes anything in its path–which explains why large trucks are sometimes called juggernauts in the UK! The word comes from the Hindu god Jagannātha meaning lord of the world. Once a year his statue is placed on a huge chariot and paraded through the streets of Puri in the Indian state of Odisha.

January

Janus was a two-faced god. What better god, therefore, to plonk right at the beginning of the year? One of his faces can look back to the old year –enjoying lovely memories and learning lessons. The other face can busily and excitedly look forward to the new year: the adventures to come, the rivers to cross, the mountains to climb.

Karaoke

If, like me, you like to sing,
Karaoke is the thing.
The word itself is Japanese
Or words, since two in one word squeeze.
First comes empty: that part's kara,
Then there's oke: orchestra.
A backing track has quite a hole
Without a trill, without a troll.
In fact it's just an empty song
Until you choose to sing along!

Etymologically speaking
The notion of **kara** or emptiness also finds its way into the form of martial arts called **karate**. In Japanese, the **kara** or **empty** is joined to **te** for **hand**. So it's down to your bare hands and feet to do the chopping, and not the weapons you grasp!
What's in a name?
Karaoke wasn't invented until 1971. At this time the coolest kids were dancing in clubs to **disco** music played by uber-cool disc jockeys or DJs. Disco is an abbreviation of **discothèque**, a French word meaning **a library of discs** (or records).
Karaoke: A form of entertainment where people sing popular songs over pre-recorded backing tracks
Word origin: Japanese
Meaning in source language: Empty orchestra

Khaki

In Urdu, khākī means dust. The dust-colored khaki fabric used to make uniforms was first worn by British troops in the 1860s to camouflage themselves against the dry landscapes of North Africa. Before this, military uniforms were designed to stand out rather than blend in, so matching the dusty backdrop was quite revolutionary.

Kayo

I include kayo because it's a very funny type of word. It's a sort of expanded **acronym** that's become a fully-fledged word. In the boxing ring, the final winning punch would result in a knockout or a KO for short. In the 1920s this acronym would be heard more than the word knockout itself. The upshot was that people started using kayo in all walks of life: "The star of the show got an ovation night after night–she was a total kayo!"

Kindergarten

Did you go to kindergarten or to a day nursery? They are very similar, but they are also etymological cousins. Kindergarten means child garden in German. It's not because of the setting but the idea of little children as plants: the need to nourish and cultivate them to get the best, brightest blooms. And, just like the young plants in a garden center or nursery, every child needs slightly different care to thrive.

Did you know?

A lobster never stops growing! There's a special word to describe this kind of creature: **accrescent**. Lizards and snakes are also accrescent.

What's in a name?

Though we humans aren't accrescent, parts of us are. Our noses and ears never stop growing! It's always more noticeable at the tip: the tip of the ear is, of course, that lovely, soft, sometimes decorated lobe. The name for the tip of the nose is the **apex**! Did you know you had an accrescent apex right in the middle of your face?

Locust

Have you seen a locust swarm?
In countries that are very warm
These insects land on farmers' fields
And munch upon their precious yields.
So might the name mean munching mobster?
No! Locusta's tiny lobster.
The Latin name they gave this hopper
(Naughty, hungry harvest-chopper!)
Annoys those shellfish who avow
There is no likeness anyhow!

Locust: A large solitary grasshopper which sometimes migrates in vast swarms to find food

Word origin: Latin

Meaning in source language: Lobster

lackluster

Lackluster is one of many Shakespearian **coinings**. We often call Shakespeare the "immortal bard" meaning the eternal poet. It is true because his word inventions are everywhere. He created a new word for dull by joining lack meaning without with luster meaning shine or sparkle and first used it in *As You Like It*, one of my favorite plays. Shakespeare loved putting "lack" in front of all kinds of words to make insults: a "lackbrain" was a foolish person, a "lacklove" an unlovable person, and a "lacklinen" was someone scruffy!

leopard

The pard was a mythological big cat. Leopards were believed to be the offspring of a male pard and a lioness. The word for this hybrid beast comes from the Greek leo and pardos (lion and pard). In fact leopards and lions (along with tigers, jaguars, snow leopards, cheetahs and cougars) are all different big-cat species. They cannot interbreed in the wild and certainly not with mythical creatures!

Leotard

Jules Léotard (1838-1870) led a celebrated but tragically short life. He was the most famous trapeze artist of his day but died of smallpox when he was only 32. "He'd fly through the air with the greatest of ease" (as the song about him said), with his wonderful torso poured into a stretchy one-piece to show off his moves. It wasn't until about 15 years after Léotard's death that his name and his most famous garment became intertwined.

Magnolia: A tree or shrub with large pink or white waxy flowers

Word origin: Named after Pierre Magnol (1638–1715)

Word first used: 18th century

Did you know?

Fossils have shown that magnolia trees existed 20 million years ago! That era is known as the **Miocene** era, from Greek **meiōn** meaning **less** and **kainos** for **new**. I'd say "less new" is a bit of an understatement for a 20-million-year-old fossil!

Magnolia

Pierre Magnol, a botanist,
Just loved to study plants:
He lived and breathed them all his life
Deep in the south of France.
In botany–and here's the thing–
A plant without a name
Can take on yours to mark your find
And bring you lots of fame.
So when the Frenchman found a tree
With flowers white and pink
The name to choose was crystal clear–
He didn't have to think!
And so we have **magnolia**–
A tribute to his deeds.
It blooms in gardens everywhere
from Winchester to Leeds!

Etymologically speaking

Another eponymous tree is the **clementine**, bearing that juicy citrus fruit that the orange regards as its sweet baby sister. It takes its name from French missionary Brother **Clément** Rodier (1839–1904), who grew and devoured them in his pretty Algerian garden!

Mackintosh

Scottish chemist Charles Macintosh (1766-1843) was a very clever man indeed. He was the first person to invent rubberized cloth which allowed people wearing it to become a sort of human duck, for rainwater simply ran off it. He was so proud of it that he gave his rubberized cloaks or mackintoshes his own name (adding a "k") in the 1830s–a name that British people still use today. Well done, Charlie!

Marathon

Today we know the marathon as a run of a very specific length: 26.2 miles to be precise. But the name comes from the story of a long journey from the plains of Marathon. Yes! A place. It was Pheidippides, in 490 BCE, who bounded the whole way to Athens with exciting news for the Greeks of their victory over the Persian army. After his exhausting dash, the notion of anything epic, including the world's most famous run, could earn the adjective marathon!

Maverick

Much to the dismay of the state of Texas, cattle farmer Samuel A. Maverick (1803-1870) refused to brand his calves. Perhaps he felt it cruel to burn a mark of ownership into their young flesh, believed in the principle of trusting one's neighbor or just didn't like being told what to do. Maverick's rebellious streak caught the imagination of the country in the late 1800s and ever since then his name has been applied to those who defy authority. Perhaps the most famous of all young mavericks was the gorgeous young man played by James Dean in the 1955 blockbuster film *Rebel Without a Cause.*

Navel: A knotty dent in a person's belly where the umbilical cord was once attached

Word origin: Old English

Meaning in source language: The middle

Navel

The English town of Naseby
Can be found upon a map.
Its name is shared with navel
And their meanings overlap!
They both come from nafela:
Old English for the middle
And to explain the reason why
Let's puzzle out this riddle!
Naseby's in the middle:
A belly-button town.
And so, just like your navel,
Is halfway up or down!

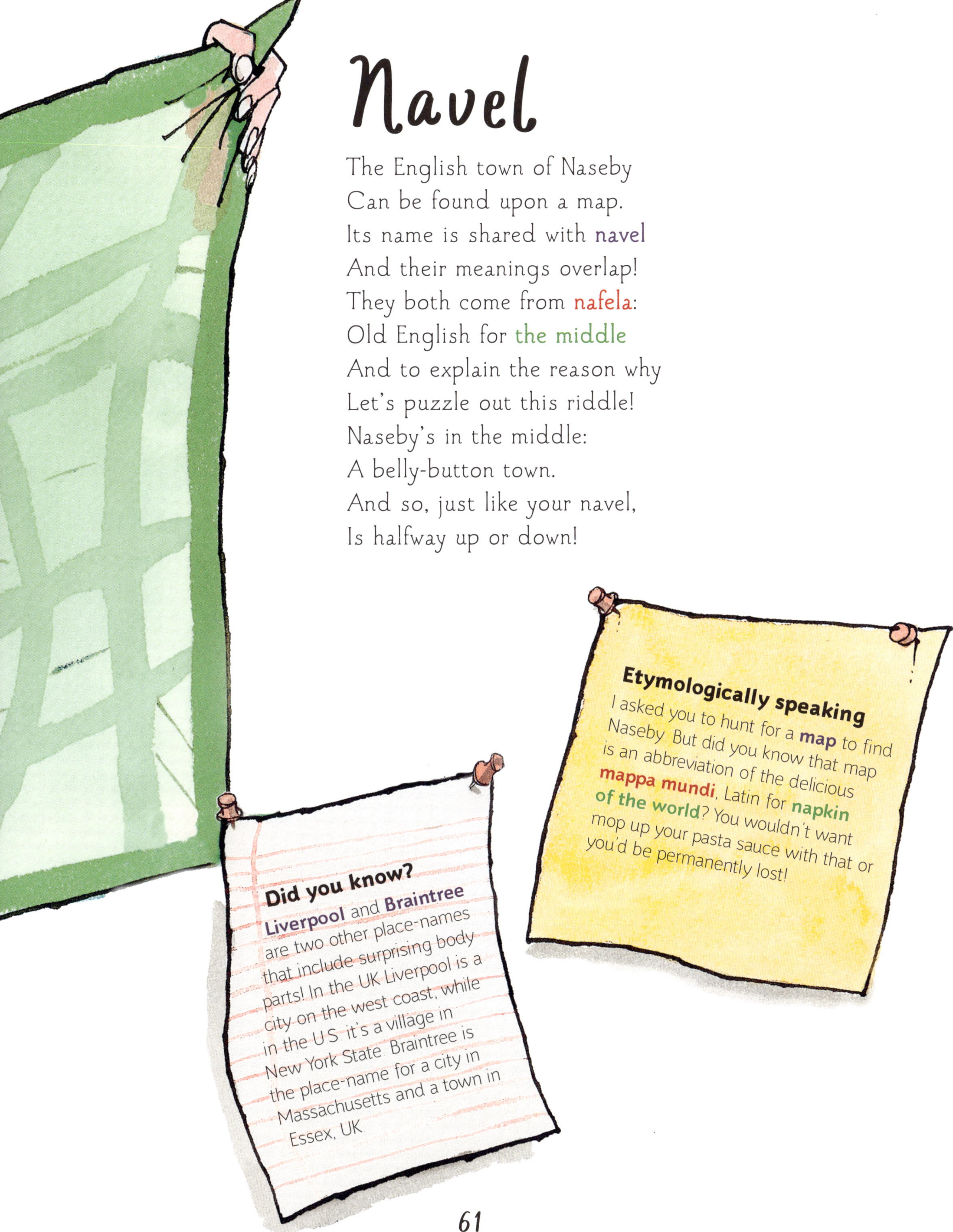

Etymologically speaking

I asked you to hunt for a **map** to find Naseby. But did you know that map is an abbreviation of the delicious **mappa mundi**, Latin for **napkin of the world**? You wouldn't want mop up your pasta sauce with that or you'd be permanently lost!

Did you know?

Liverpool and **Braintree** are two other place-names that include surprising body parts! In the UK Liverpool is a city on the west coast, while in the US it's a village in New York State. Braintree is the place-name for a city in Massachusetts and a town in Essex, UK.

Nurse

Nurse is one of those words that appears everywhere. When you were a baby, someone fed or "nursed" you every time you were hungry. Later your curiosity may have been nourished at a day nursery. If you have a garden, your flowers might have first been nursed in a nursery. If you've ever had to go to the hospital, you will have been nursed by a medical nurse. With all these examples, the golden thread that binds them is feeding, which is where the word comes from–nutricius is Latin for a person that nourishes.

Neon

You may have heard "neo" popping up here and there if you are into the arts. In music, for example, there is neo soul, neo jazz, and neo funk. It simply means new from the Greek neon. In terms of gases, neon was very late to the party, not discovered until 1898 by Sir William Ramsay and Morris W. Travers, who felt neon was a fitting name for this gas with its reddish-orange glow.

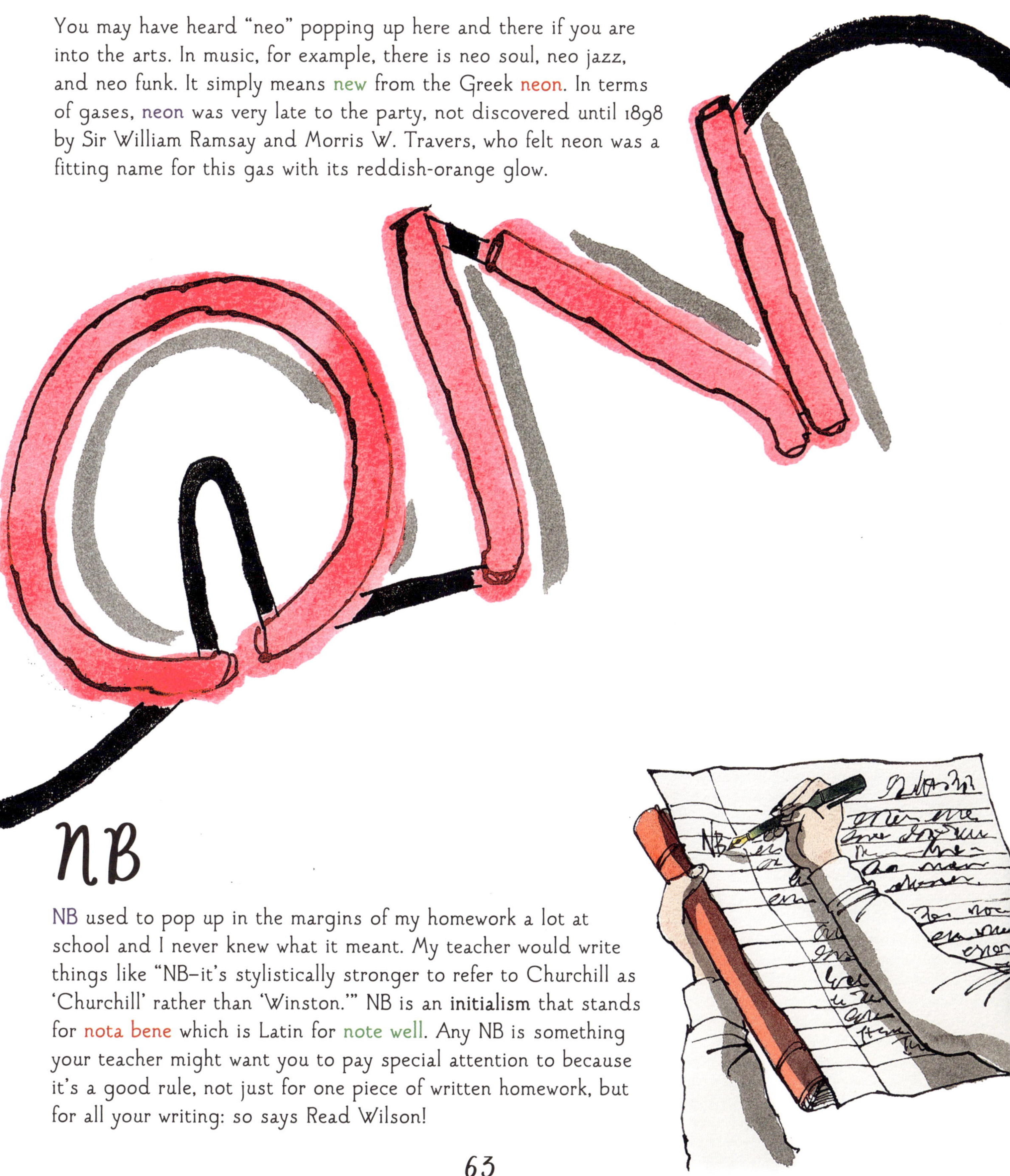

NB

NB used to pop up in the margins of my homework a lot at school and I never knew what it meant. My teacher would write things like "NB–it's stylistically stronger to refer to Churchill as 'Churchill' rather than 'Winston.'" NB is an **initialism** that stands for nota bene which is Latin for note well. Any NB is something your teacher might want you to pay special attention to because it's a good rule, not just for one piece of written homework, but for all your writing: so says Read Wilson!

Octopus

It strikes me as funny–by which I mean odd–
That mollusks like this have no feet.
The octo and pus suggest there are eight
To render each leg complete!
Yes, they have suckers and yes, they grow back–
If ravenous sharks bite them off
But eight cheesy, sock-wearing, flat-bottomed ends
If they *were* there, have now all dropped off!

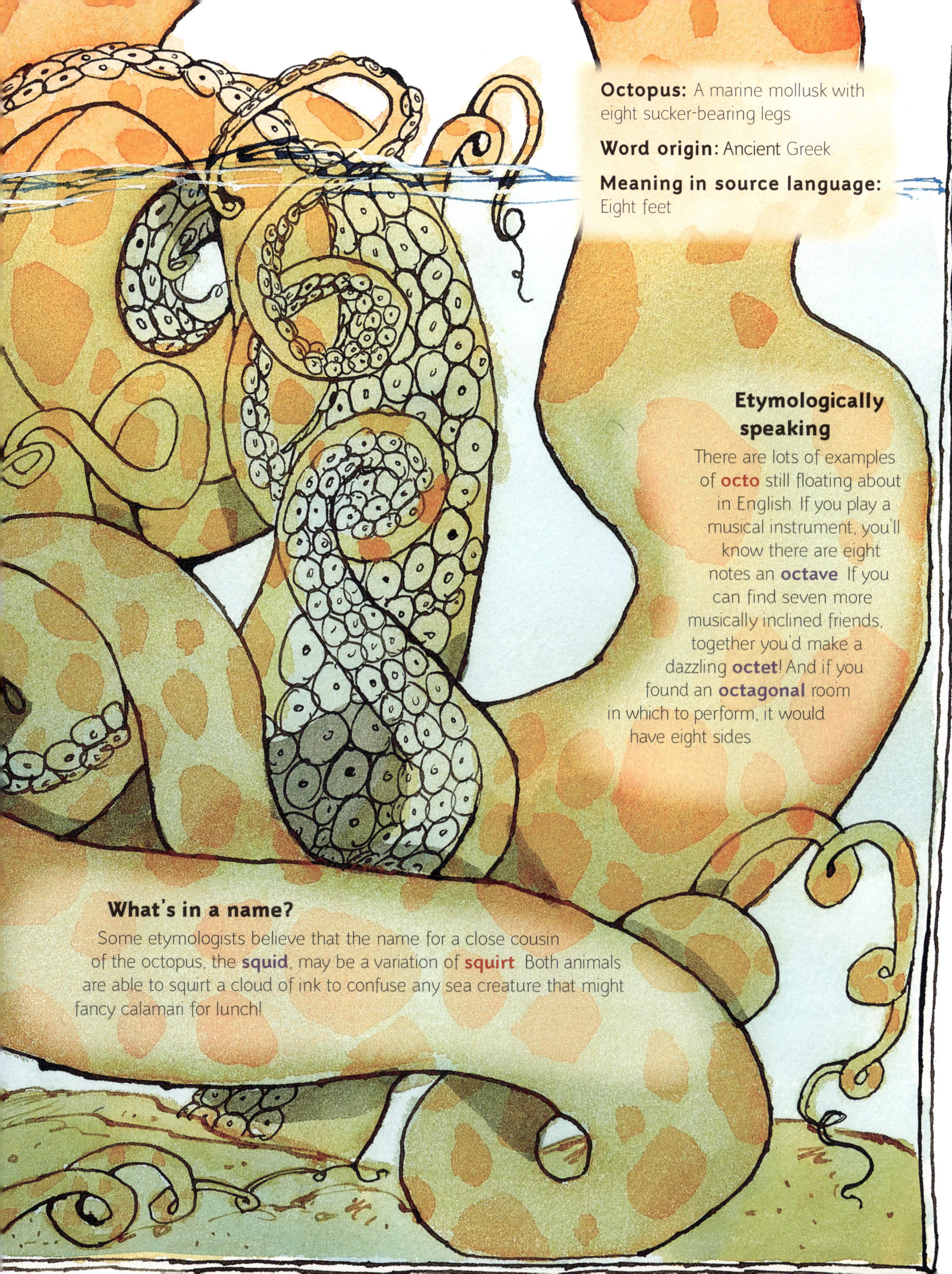

Octopus: A marine mollusk with eight sucker-bearing legs

Word origin: Ancient Greek

Meaning in source language: Eight feet

Etymologically speaking

There are lots of examples of **octo** still floating about in English. If you play a musical instrument, you'll know there are eight notes an **octave**. If you can find seven more musically inclined friends, together you'd make a dazzling **octet**! And if you found an **octagonal** room in which to perform, it would have eight sides.

What's in a name?

Some etymologists believe that the name for a close cousin of the octopus, the **squid**, may be a variation of **squirt**. Both animals are able to squirt a cloud of ink to confuse any sea creature that might fancy calamari for lunch!

Ogre

I don't know about you, but when I think of an ogre I instantly think of Shrek. I think of it as another word for giant, really. But its etymology is much scarier than giant, which simply means, well, giant. Ogre is probably from the Italian ocra meaning demon or monster, which explains why you've never heard of the BFO or Big Friendly Ogre. I suppose the friendliest ogre would be Shrek, although he can be pretty grumpy!

Oubliette

Oublier is French for to forget. In medieval castles, an oubliette was a secret dungeon accessed by a trapdoor. The oubliette was actively forgotten because nothing in the room above it advertised its presence. This made the dungeon most effective when it was needed to imprison an enemy!

Omnibus

Did you know that the bus was lopped off the end of this word? The full word, omnibus, comes from the French voiture omnibus meaning carriage for all. The omni or all was much more important to stress in the early 1800s because the idea of affordable transportation for the poor was very new. When it became expected that everybody could hop onto the omnibus, the "omni" part started to be taken for granted, so instead people simply caught the bus.

Pajamas: A loose-fitting shirt and matching pants for sleeping in

Word origin: Persian

Meaning in source language: Leg clothing

Pajamas

Pajamas come from Persia, and from its language too:
That pae means leg and jamah clothes is what I'm telling you!
The garment looked like trousers, loose and very light,
Woven from the finest silks–a most becoming sight!
As pajamas traveled west, the merchants often said
That legwear so delectable was great to wear in bed.
Indeed the floaty bottom half was perfect in a bunk,
But what about above the waist? A naked, chilly trunk!
And so for colder climes like ours–for frosty night-time air–
A top to join the bottoms and make a matching pair!

Did you know?

If someone calls you **the cat's pajamas** they mean you're **the bee's knees** or **the elephant's ears** sorry, it's addictive! They mean you're the best. These animal-centric compliments were all the rage in 1920s America!

Piranha

This word is as scary as the leg-nibbling animal it describes. Piranha comes from Tupi, a Brazilian language: pirá means fish and sainha is tooth. Piranhas are aptly named since they have very powerful jaws, home to razor-sharp teeth that can regrow multiple times over their lifespan!

Phlegmatic

The Ancient Greek doctor Hippocrates believed that human health was connected to the balance of four bodily fluids that he called humors: blood, black bile, yellow bile, and phlegm (or snot). Too much snot, for Hippocrates, didn't make a very leaky person but a very relaxed person. I suppose all the gooey stickiness of excess snot would weigh you down and slow you down. This gives the old-fashioned and rather yucky word phlegmatic–almost excessively relaxed.

Porridge

What do you add to your oatmeal? Brown sugar? Banana? Leek? Yes, leek! Not as wild a choice as you might think, because oatmeal is a type of porridge and that's where porridge gets its name. The Old French porée means leek soup, from the Latin porrum for leek. What porridge and leek soup have in common is that they start with a lot of liquid and enjoy a slow, steady reduction over a flame, into a lovely thick consistency.

Quignog

Never dismiss a quignog!
Quignogs will help you to strive.
In fact, the quignogs you harbor
Must always be kept alive!
Roughly translating as pipe dreams
From the Cornish **vernacular**,
Whether it's Broadway or spaceflight you're chasing
I bet your quignog's spectacular!
Mine was to write this book:
To share lovely words with you
And since it is here before your eyes
I guess some quignogs come true!

Etymologically speaking

Cornwall probably comes from the Celtic name **Cornowii** which likely means **the people of the horn**, since they live on the horn of the island!

Did you know?

Cornwall is the region at the very southwestern tip of the island of Great Britain If you were to go there today and throw the biggest tantrum you have ever thrown, a local may call you a **heller** A special word reserved for children who make a sizeable scene!

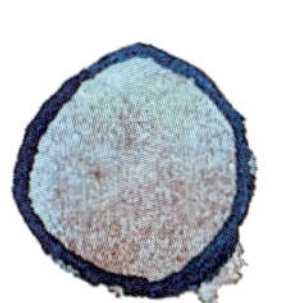

Quignog: An aspiration or dream

Word origin: Cornish **dialect**

Meaning in source language: A ridiculous notion

Quafftide

Quaffing is my favorite word for having a drink and the word is perhaps an imitation of the sound we make when we swallow. You can quaff anything from lemonade to champagne, but when we speak of quafftide, it takes on quite boozy connotations. It's that time in the evening, perhaps 7 p.m., when any grown-ups in your life may decide that they'd like a small glass of wine, a beer, or some such (and here's another favorite word of mine) tipple. Tide, by the way, is a very attractive old synonym for time.

Quarantine

We have learned from coronavirus that quarantines are very stretchy things. Their length changes depending on risk levels. But quarantine actually has a very specific time frame built into its name. It comes from the Italian Venetian dialect word quarantena or 40 days. In the 14th century Venice introduced a law requiring ships from plague-ridden countries to wait for 40 days before they could enter the port. This period would help keep the plague from getting off the ship and being spread all over Venice like marmalade.

Queensland

The Australian state of Queensland takes its name not from Queen Elizabeth II, but from her great-great-grandmother, Queen Victoria. The first British settlers in Australia established a colony in the 18th century which they called New South Wales. In 1859, 22 years into her reign, Queen Victoria created a separate state from the northern part of New South Wales and it was named as Queensland in her honor. Queensland is incredibly huge–bigger than the state of Alaska!

Rhinoceros

If I said, "Wipe your rhino," you might think that was weird
Or even that my common sense had totally disappeared!
But what if then I told you rhino's Ancient Greek for nose?
I think that you would understand what every wordsmith knows:
Rhinoceros–in full, of course–a horn-nosed herbivore.
And rhinos dig up plants to eat–that's what the horn is for!

Rhinoceros: A large plant-eating mammal with one or two horns on its nose, native to Africa and parts of Asia

Word origin: Ancient Greek

Meaning in source language: Horn-nosed

Did you know?

Rhinos can produce 50 pounds of poop every day That's a very big pile! And, interestingly, **dung** (the polite word for poop) comes from the Danish **dynga** meaning **heap**

Ritzy

In 1906 Monsieur César Ritz (1850-1918) opened the doors of his first luxury hotel in Paris. It was so successful that Ritz Hotels in London and New York soon followed. By 1926 his hotels were so famous for stylish extravagance that ritzy was used to describe anything expensive and glamorous. The word was turned into a phrase–"puttin' on the ritz"–that became the title of a hit song. It was made famous when it was performed in the 1946 film *Blue Skies* by Fred Astaire.

Robot

A mechanical person, forced to work so we don't have to. That doesn't sound like the kindest description of a robot but that is exactly what its name means, from the Czech robota or forced labor. I prefer android, a slightly friendlier name for a robot, that comes from Ancient Greek and means "like a man."

Rupee

The rupee is a currency used across Asia and is as old as it is widespread. It dates back to around 300 BCE and its name comes from the Sanskrit rūpa meaning beautiful form. It was very aptly named. If you have time, look up some early rupees on the internet. They are works of art that carry perfectly formed lettering and beautiful images.

Shampoo

Rub-a-dub-dub, you're in the tub,
Having a soak and a brush and a scrub.
And, as you lather your beautiful tresses,
It's not your shampoo, but your delicate presses
That gave us this ancient Hindi word.
The meaning of champo has slowly transferred
From kneading and gently massaging your head
To the liquid you use when you do it instead!

Shampoo: A foamy preparation for washing the hair

Word origin: Hindi—a language spoken in India

Meaning in source language: To press

Did you know?

Bottled shampoo didn't exist until 1930, thanks to American Dr. John H Breck. Before the use of manufactured shampoo, people would rub-a-dub-dub their hair with soap made from oil and soda. Once a month they might wash their hair with eggs!!

Etymologically speaking

My daddy is a sailor. He was in fact nominated for the BBC's Sports Personality of the Year in 1979. He sailed *Fireballs*: a type of **dinghy** named for its immense speed. I tell you all of this not (well not just) to show off about Daddy, but because dinghy is another Hindi word, from **dinghi** meaning **small boat**.

Salary

What do salaries and sausages have in common? Not much at first glance but sausages (which were nicknamed "bags of mystery" in 19th century England for their dubious contents) were always salted and take their name from the Latin for salty–salsus. Salary, similarly, is from the Latin salarium which was salt-money, a Roman soldier's allowance to buy salt. At a time when salt was essential for the flavoring and preservation of food, it was a very natural nickname for a basic wage. Basic wages have, ever since, been linked to food: think "breadwinner" and "bringing home the bacon!"

Squirrel

These city chums of mine aren't at all like the squirrels I remember as a small child. Those country squirrels would zip into the canopy of the nearest oak if you came anywhere near them. My furry friends in Brompton Cemetery come and chat as though eager to help me with my crossword puzzle. All the while the sun filters through their showy tails making pretty patterns on the ground. And that tail shadow gives them their name since skia is Greek for shadow and oura is tail.

Sideburns

This is a most unique word because it is a sort of eponymous flip-flop. Ambrose Burnside (1824–1881) was a Union General in the American Civil War. If you look at his severe yet handsome face, you'll see he sports enormous sideburns that have become so chummy with his moustache, they've actually joined hands! His magnificent facial hair might have resulted in a straight eponym, but was flip-flopped because of the location of the growth: on each *side* of his face.

Tango

The tango is a steamy dance
That has a Latin beat.
But who was first to name it
And try it with their feet?
The people of Ibibio
From Africa's western shore
Loved to tamgu–meaning dance–
Across a dusty floor.
It's now a ballroom favorite–
As raunchy as can be–
Full of fancy footwork...
And sensuality!

Tango: A dance characterized by marked rhythms and postures and abrupt pauses

Word origin: Ibibio – a dialect spoken in parts of West Africa

Meaning in source language: To dance

What's in a name?

My favorite dance, the **polka**, shares something with the tango insofar as the name is more generic The dance became popular in 19th century Bohemia and comes from the Polish word for **Polish woman** —**Polka** Of course, just because the dance is called a polka doesn't mean you have to scoop up a girl Your partner can be anyone you choose!

Etymologically speaking

Most ballroom dance names contain an instruction as to what the step actually is: the **paso doble** comes from the Spanish for **double step**, the **waltz** is from the German **waltzen** meaning **revolve**, and the **quickstep** is exactly what it says on the label!

Tulip

There are two things in the world, now that diapers aren't folded, that are to my mind the most beautifully wrapped things. One is a closed tulip. The intricately folded petals are almost as pretty as the open flower. The other is a turban, where the careful intertwined wrapping is responsible for its shape and beauty. And these two things are cousins! Tulbent is the Turkish word for turban and, without it, the word tulip wouldn't exist.

Taxidermy

Taxis, in Greek, did not mean those cabs with a light that turns on when they are free to hire, but arrangement. Derma is the Greek for skin (which is why we call skin doctors dermatologists). Taxidermy is therefore the art of arranging the skin of dead animals around lots of stuffing to make them resemble their shape and form when they were alive! In the 19th century, before either television or air travel, stuffed animals were displayed for the scientific study of exotic species. Many of them survive in the glass cabinets of our museums today.

Teddy bear

Talking of stuffed animals, the cuddly teddy bear gets its name from President Theodore Roosevelt (1858-1919), who was known as Teddy. He lived at a time when bear hunting was a popular pastime but on one particular outing in 1902 the president refused to shoot a bear that had been cornered by his aides. A businessman named Morris Michtom saw the commercial opportunity and began to make and sell plush toys that he called "Teddy's Bears," dedicated to the president. And so the teddy bear was born!

Umbo

On nearly every shield of old there is a central knob;
A circular, protruding bit–a lumpy metal blob.
If I informed you that the knob is labeled as an **umbo**
You might believe I'd made it up or say it's mumbo jumbo!
But truly, almost everything you see has its own name
Even sticky-outy bits–and you know who's to blame?
Who has over-classified, is on a wordy misson?
The Romans: who just love to give each thing a definition!

What's in a name?

Once upon a time a suit of armor was called a **coat of mail.** This did not mean a jacket made of old postcards but instead used the Old French **maille** from the Latin **macula** meaning mesh. Literally, a tunic of metal **mesh**. Comfy!

Etymologically speaking

The umbo is the only sticky-outy part of a suit of armor that isn't made to cover one of our own sticky-outy parts! The other sticky-outy pieces are the **couter**—designed for our sticky-outy elbows, and the **poleyn**—designed for our sticky-outy knees. Both come from Old French, where **poullain** meant **knee**, and **coute** meant **elbow**.

Umbo: A stud or boss on the center of a shield

Word origin: Latin

Meaning in source language: Shield boss

Umbrella

Sunshades made from palm leaves or peacock feathers have been used since ancient times. In the 17th century the Italians began to apply wax to their ombrelli (from the Latin umbra meaning shade). With this change in design the handheld canopies or umbrellas became more about protection from the rain than from the sun.

Uranus

Uranus was the Greek god of the sky. The German astronomer Johann Elert Bode contributed to the discovery of Uranus in 1781 and suggested the name for the planet to continue a naming system that had been in place since ancient times. Mercury, Venus, Mars, Jupiter, and Saturn can all be seen with the naked eye and so have been known about for millennia. In Roman mythology Saturn is Jupiter's father. The idea was the kindly Saturn placed his son nearer to the Sun to encourage him to grow. So Bode thought Saturn's father and Jupiter's grandfather, Uranus, would surely have done the same.

Ursula

When I hear the name Ursula I automatically think of my favorite Disney villain: that heavily eye-shadowed, bassoon-voiced, lilac sea witch in *The Little Mermaid*. The name comes from the Latin ursa meaning, no, not giant octopus, but bear. Ursa gives us the lovely word ursine, meaning bear-like. Hans Christian Andersen, who wrote the original fairy tale of *The Little Mermaid*, didn't name his sea witch so Ursula was coined by the Disney film. I suppose the idea was she was the grizzly bear of the sea with a ferocious roar, an imposing frame, and oodles of power.

Vermin

Vermin, like pigeons and rats, can be smelly
And, as a word, looks like "vermicelli!"
Instead of referring to rats spreading germs
The Latin word vermis simply meant worms!
No wonder that pasta, all slippy and thin,
Found the word vermis (or worms) creeping in.
I don't mean, of course, real worms in your belly
But worms in the word to make vermicelli.

Vermin: Animals that are harmful to crops, livestock, or property, or that carry disease

Word origin: Latin

Meaning in source language: Worm

Here's one variety act that never ceases to amaze me–the ventriloquist and dummy. Let's break the word down: it comes from the Latin venter meaning belly and loqui meaning to speak. The idea of speaking from the belly was originally connected with a rather dark art where the ventriloquist was thought to have an unliving spirit in their stomach and was therefore able to communicate with the dead. It was only later, in the 19th century, that ventriloquist was the name given to a performer who had honed the skill of generating a voice for their puppet from the belly without moving the lips and jaw. A sort of human bagpipe!

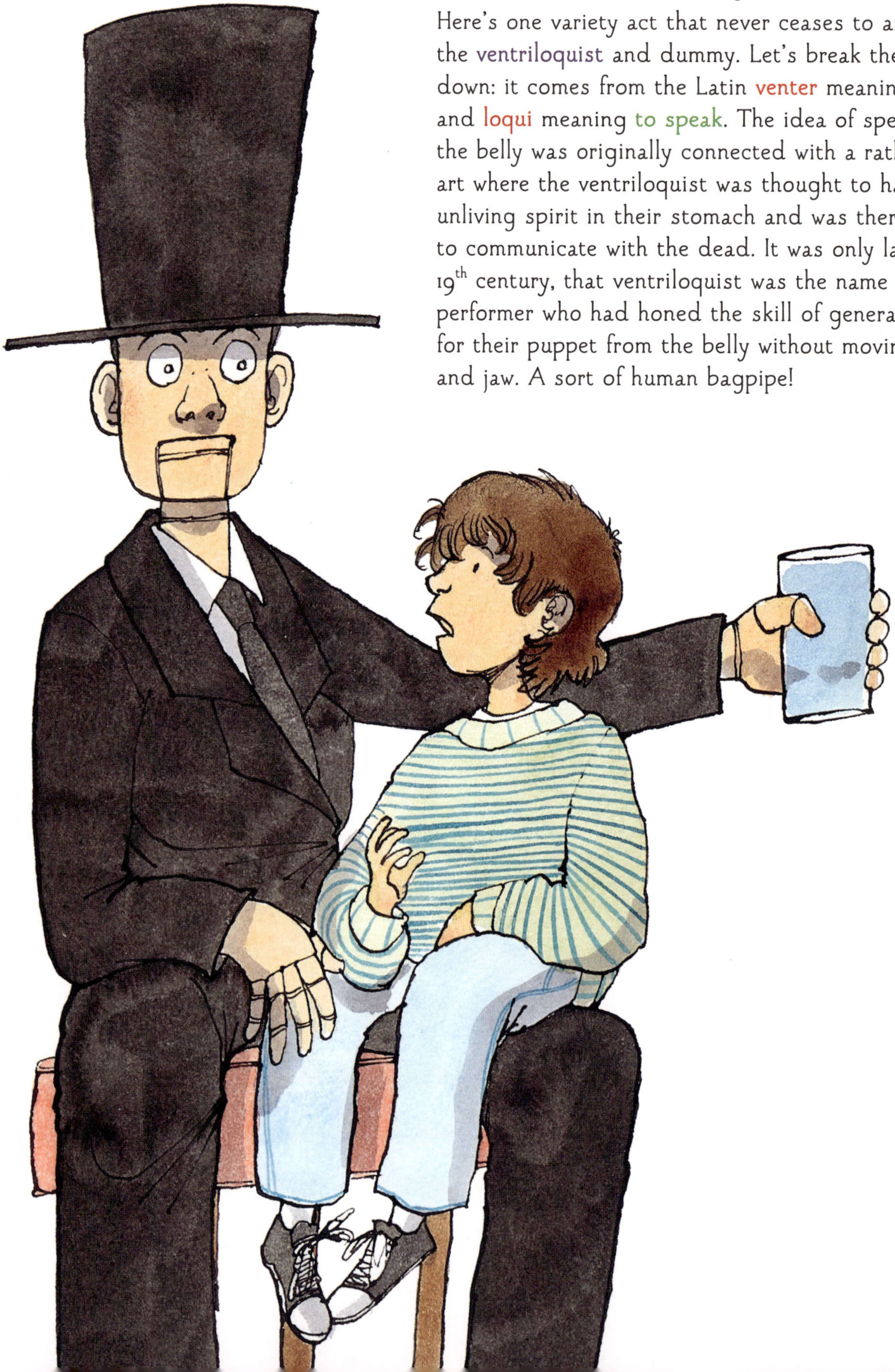

Vindaloo

The fiery curry we call vindaloo started out as a milder Portuguese dish of meat marinated in wine vinegar and garlic or vinha d'alhos. It traveled with Portuguese sailors to India, where the ingredients were tweaked according to what was available locally–tamarind, pepper, and chilies. The resulting dish had a similar sounding name but wow, it packs a hot, hot punch!

Volt

Did you know the first electric battery was invented in 1800? And by whom? You guessed it! A Mr. Volt. Well, Count Alessandro Volta (1745-1827) to be precise. Volta lived in Como in Italy and was a scientist. Earlier scientific experiments had shown that electrical current could be passed through the legs of a dissected frog to make them move, but Volta proved that two different metals and some acid was all that was needed to create an electrical charge.

Did you know?

The other place that's said to be very windy is our bottoms The small gusts of wind produced there are called **farts** This probably goes back to the Sanskrit **pard**: a word designed to imitate the sound of your small gusts of wind These sound words are known as **onomatopoeia**

Etymologically speaking

In Victorian Britain servants were sometimes called fart-catchers They would follow a master or mistress so attentively and with such bowed heads that they would be close enough to catch their employers' farts!

Window

Window first meant the wind's eye
Bear with me and I'll tell you why.
In olden days the window's job
Was not to stop the tempest's throb
But to be a hole that let
Winds inside, and yes, the wet!
Vandr augr in Old Norse
Is the wind's eye, and so, of course,
Ventilation comes from vandr.
And to speak with total candor,
Though a window made of glass is
Great once sunny weather passes,
When it's back you will decide
To throw your wind eye open wide.

Window: An opening in a wall, roof or vehicle, fitted with glass in a frame
Word origin: Old Norse
Meaning in source language: Wind's eye

Wendy house

To us it's a humble playhouse, but to our British friends it has a much more whimsical name—a Wendy house. It comes from J.M. Barrie's *Peter Pan*, in which Wendy Darling is shot by one of the Lost Boys and they decide to build her a little house to help her recover.

Wellingtons

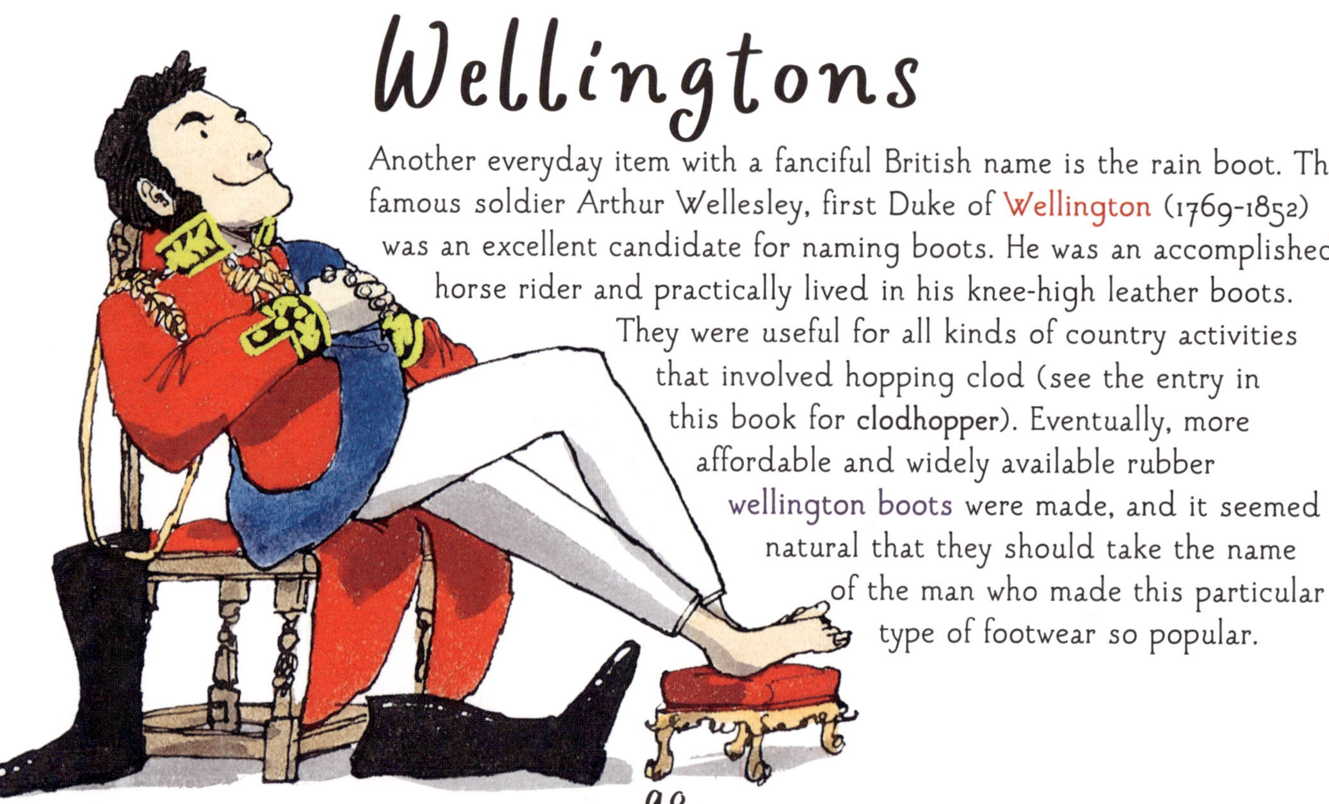

Another everyday item with a fanciful British name is the rain boot. The famous soldier Arthur Wellesley, first Duke of Wellington (1769-1852) was an excellent candidate for naming boots. He was an accomplished horse rider and practically lived in his knee-high leather boots. They were useful for all kinds of country activities that involved hopping clod (see the entry in this book for **clodhopper**). Eventually, more affordable and widely available rubber wellington boots were made, and it seemed natural that they should take the name of the man who made this particular type of footwear so popular.

Wig

Funnily enough, perruque is a French word meaning natural head of hair. This word got twisted into periwig in English, and when I say twisted I don't just mean in spelling but in meaning, too. It came to mean an artificial head of hair worn in the 17th century for status or profession. Then, just like it sometimes happens with hair, half the word got chopped off and we kept just the wig.

Xylophone

When you hear a xylophone
Today its bright and hollow tone
Reverberates from fiberglass
Which makes its name a real farce!
Xylon is the Greek for wood
(Bamboo or maple would be good).
Phonos can mean voice or sound:
A "wooden choir" that will astound.
So should an old xylophonist
The modern instrument resist?
And think the choir is just no good
Because its voice comes not from wood?

Xylophone: A musical instrument played by striking resonant bars of graduated length with one or more small wooden or plastic beaters

Word origin: Greek

Meaning in source language: Sound or voice of wood

Etymologically speaking

Xylon is **wood** and **phagous** is **eating**, so **xylophagous** animals (including beavers, deer, and termites) all eat wood. I am sure their diet is tastier than that of **coprophagous** animals—since **copros** is **poop**!

hat's in a name?

ecause the most famous oprophagous animal needed to have his fact woven into its name, we kindly chose the slightly more elegant dung for the dung beetle. It reportedly wasn't wild about turd beetle, poo beetle, or number two beetle.

Xenon

Xenon is a gas that is extremely useful. It can be used in everything from anesthetic to electric light. Such a versatile gas has an almost magical quality, which may be how it gets its name, from the Greek root xenos meaning strange. Luckily, here, we're not insulting xenon but acknowledging that it's rather weird and wonderful.

Xerox

Xerox is a super word to say, but it is only half of the lovely xerography. The word, meaning dry writing in Greek, was a printing process invented in 1938 by American physicist Chester Carlson (1906-1968) using powdered instead of liquid ink to stop trickling and smearing. Ten years later the word xerox was coined by the company that adopted Carlson's invention as a method of photocopying.

X-ray

In 1895 German engineer Wilhelm Röntgen (1845-1923) discovered rays with a shorter wavelength than visible light rays. He called them X-Strahlen which translates as X-rays, the "X" denoting that the nature of these rays was unknown. We now know all about X-rays but the name has stuck!

Yogurt

Adding to yogurt is par for the course:
Raspberries, blueberries...Worcestershire sauce!
The word comes from Turkish that sounded like "yort"
(The "ğ" with its accent an unspoken sort).
When turned into English the "g" was restored
Something the Turks might have simply abhorred!
Yoğurt translates as condense, which is true:
When milk starts to curdle it turns into goo!
Next time you eat it, add pickles, add brie!
But would you–for fun–just try dropping the "g?"

Whats in a name?

Yogurt is just one kind of fermented food to enjoy Another is **sauerkraut**—cabbage that has been finely chopped and pickled We've borrowed the word from the German **sauerkraut** which means **sour vegetable**

Did you know?

Although yogurt has been eaten for more than 5,000 years, frozen yogurt was not introduced until the 1970s when an American food company began to sell a new product marketed as "frogurt"

Yogurt: A food prepared from milk (or plant-based alternatives) fermented by adding healthy bacteria and often flavored or sweetened

Word origin: Turkish

Meaning in source language: Condensed

Yard

Orchard comes from the Old English ortgeard. The geard part of the word gave us yard and garden–they stem from the same root. And the words are still cousins today: you might have a back garden if you live on one side of the Atlantic Ocean, while on the other side the same space is your backyard.

"Lay ee odl lay ee odl-oo"

Yodel

"High on a hill was a lonely goatherd
Lay ee odl lay ee odl lay hee hoo
Loud was the voice of the lonely goatherd
Lay ee odl lay ee odl-oo." - Oscar Hammerstein II

That's what yodeling looks like on paper. The sound, however, is one of intense joy and jo, pronounced "yo" in German, is and was an exclamation of joy. So this joy singing earned the name jodeln.

Yeti

In lexical terms yeti is the little brother of the abominable snowman. The Tibetan word combines gya and dred or rocky and bear to make this terrible hairy creature of the Himalayas: 50 percent man, 50 percent bear, 100 percent terrifying!

Zombie: An undead monster said to be a corpse revived by witchcraft

Word origin: Kikongo—a language spoken in parts of West Africa

Meaning in source language: The name of a voodoo serpent god

Zombie

Those creepy monsters that we fear started as a name
For Zombi was a serpent god of mystic voodoo fame.
His powers were supernatural, and some have even said
His magical abilities were used to raise the dead!
Hence zombies: those great spooky things that make you want to hide
With horrid arms outstretched and their bodies mummified!
If you're scared, I understand, but I should let you know–
A zombie seldom catches you–they can't–they're far too slow!

Did you know?

Zombies fall under the large umbrella term of **phantoms** Also under this umbrella are ghosts, spirits, and spooks Mercifully for all of our heart rates, phantom comes from the Greek **phantasma** meaning **apparition** or **mere image** so we don't have to worry The etymology suggests they are all illusions

What's in a name?

Phantasma has produced some much lovelier words: **phantasmagorical** and **fantastic** are both really the stuff of our imaginations or **fantasy**

Zither

A zither is an ancient sort of guitar. Arguably, the earliest kind of guitar is a sort of lap harp called the lyre. The entry-level, seven-stringed lyre was great as a starting point for any future string master! This was called the kithara. The beautiful lap kithara inspired the eventual lap zither, though the zither is far trickier to navigate! Zither, guitar, and kithara can all trace their word stories back to the Latin cithara meaning harp.

Zodiac

The great Babylonians were responsible for what we call star signs. They basically chopped up the cosmos or heavens into 12 and gave each section an animal sign, apart from Libra which means balance and is represented as weighing scales. The whole collection of animals is called the zodiac, from the Greek zōidiakòs kýklos meaning circle of little animals!

Zoo

The Zoological Society of London–devoted to the study of animals (from two lovely Greek words: zoion for animals and logia for study)–established a public collection of wild animals in Regent's Park in 1829. These Zoological Gardens were quickly abbreviated to "the Zoological" and then shortened further to "the Zoo." The word's origins are perfect, since to run a happy zoo the keepers must know the behaviors and habits of their animals very well indeed.

TOM READ WILSON

My love affair with words goes back to my earliest childhood. My father was an English teacher before he retired and he devoured books. I have so many fond memories of the pleasure he took in using words, saying things like, "well, this has been lovely, but all too brief, fleeting, short-lived, ephemeral." My mother was also an inspiration. As a fine amateur actress, she encouraged me to take to the stage. At school I discovered Rodgers and Hammerstein and was bewitched by their music and the perfect rhymes of their poignant lyrics.

After leaving school I attended Rose Bruford College and the Royal Academy of Music where I learned that everything I needed to be a performer could be found in the lines or lyrics–that is to say, in the words themselves.

Today I work more in television than in theater but I still recite a Shakespearian sonnet every morning and night to keep my life's libretto as zestful as it was in my acting days. Whether we are performers or not, words are our universal currency and they enrich our souls and our lives.

IAN MORRIS

Drawing runs in the Morris family. My granddad was highly recommended by his teacher to go to art school. However, he was from a poor area of Manchester where aspirations of being an artist had no place and was told to get a "proper" job. Yet he was a great inspiration, buying me a *Beano* and *Dandy* comic book each week. They influenced the early compositional narratives that I devised in my own comics. When I was eight years old I discovered *The Edge Chronicles* and was lost in the elegant line work and dynamic compositions of Chris Riddell's illustrations. That was the moment I knew I wanted to be an illustrator. I had the pleasure of meeting Chris twice before my career started to gain traction and he kindly endorsed my first picture book, *The Library Book*.

Now, as an illustrator, one of the Morris family has finally put their artistic flair to good use! This book has been a dream project: it has pushed my creativity and allowed me to develop my visual style. My compelling ambition is to make beautifully illustrated books.